Introduction to

FINANCIAL
STEWARDSHIP

GW00686305

Andrew Wommack

Published in partnership between Andrew Wommack Ministries and Harrison House Publishers.

Woodland Park, CO 80863 – Shippensburg, PA 17257

ISBN 13 TP: 978-1-59548-633-2

For Worldwide Distribution, Printed in the USA

1 2 3 4 5 6 / 26 25 24 23

CONTENTS

INTRODUCTION

You may think the most common topic Jesus spoke on was faith or prayer or love. While those certainly were part of many of His sermons, He taught more on finances than anything else. Specifically, He taught about *stewarding* finances. That puts the topic of money at a higher level of importance than I'm sure many people realize.

One of the reasons we as the church haven't made a bigger impact on modern society is because we haven't successfully applied God's principles to everything He has entrusted us with. This is especially true with finances. Most people have no idea how to steward the resources God has given them for everyday life.

I know money can be a sore subject for people. Some people get offended when ministers even talk about money. The reason for this is there has been a lot of wrong teaching, usually motivated by greed, regarding finances.

But did you know that God views stewarding your finances as basic Christianity? Jesus said that if you can't be faithful in your finances, then you can't be trusted with anything else (Luke 16:11).

Not surprisingly, what the Bible has to say about financial stewardship is different from most of what you will hear from other sources. God doesn't operate according to this world's system and economy. Operating in God's kingdom will give you an advantage, so it's important to understand how to do things His way.

In this booklet, I'm going to teach you scriptural and spiritual principles that govern finances. I'll be answering questions like . . .

- What is a steward?
- What is the proper way to give?
- What is prosperity?

As I have learned to properly apply these principles, I've seen radical change in my life and ministry. You never would have heard of me if I hadn't understood what I will be sharing with you. If you'll accept these truths, you will be the steward God wants you to be, and you will prosper—but not just in the area of finances. Every area of your life will be blessed. It all starts with having the right motive. It's the first step!

Chapter 1

Being a Steward

It's typical for Christians to groan whenever preachers start talking about money. Most people think they only do it for their own benefit. Sad to say, they are justified in thinking this way. But as I mentioned in the Introduction, Jesus taught more on finances than anything else. I guarantee you: He didn't do it for selfish purposes.

When I teach anything that the Lord has revealed to me—whether finances or emotions or healing—it's never because I'm looking to receive in those areas; it's always because I want to share what I believe will help you.

From Owner to Steward

The very first thing we need to understand about finances is that we are stewards of what God has given us. A steward is a person who manages the assets, especially the financial affairs, of another. As stewards, we need to recognize that the money we have is not really ours; it's what God has given us to manage.

You may be thinking, *I can guarantee you God didn't give me the money I have! I've worked hard for it. I've earned it.* Maybe you work two jobs, or you have scrimped for years to get a little savings, so the money you've accumulated seems like the result of your own efforts. I understand that way of thinking, but in reality, it isn't true.

Every good and perfect gift comes from God (James 1:17). Ultimately, God is the source of everything you have. First of all, He gave you life. You didn't cause yourself to exist—you were created. You have nothing that you did not receive (1 Cor. 4:7 and Rom. 11:35–36). King David said, "*. . . of thine own have we given thee*" (1 Chr. 29:14).

Most Christians say they know God is the source of everything, but their lives don't reflect an understanding of that truth. I was in a meeting one time when the man receiving the offering told everyone to reach into the back pocket or the purse of the person in front of them and "give like you've always wanted to give." Of course, no one actually did it. The point he was making is that we are much more likely to be generous with someone else's money. Most people would probably take more money from their neighbor's wallet to put in the offering than they would from their own.

When you think that money comes by your own sweat and tears, then you keep a much tighter hold on it. You become attached to your money, and it actually becomes your master. But when you see yourself as a steward and recognize that your money belongs to God, it totally changes the role it plays in your life. It no longer controls you and takes its intended place as a tool. This simple change in mindset is vastly different from the world's, but it makes all the difference!

You may have made a firm commitment to the Lord concerning spiritual things, but when it comes to money, you see it as a private possession, where God has little to no say. But He needs to be Lord over *all* of your life. Instead of seeing yourself as the owner, you need to think, *I am a steward of what God has entrusted to me. God has blessed me with these talents and abilities. God has blessed me with my job. God has given me all of the resources I have. It is not up to me to run my finances the way I want.*

Until we have this mindset, nothing else the Bible says about finances or anything else is going to work. We have to see ourselves as stewards of God's resources. We can't violate this and hope to prosper.

HAVING THE RIGHT HEART

It would be irresponsible of me to teach you how to get money without first dealing with the motive behind it. The world teaches you to "get all you can, can all you get, and then sit on your can." If you're going to prosper God's way, it's just the opposite. It's not enough that God is the source of your resources; you have to *recognize* Him as the source of your resources.

This doesn't mean you sit at home and do nothing. When you recognize that you're a steward, you do what He tells you to do, and the Bible says that *"if any would not work, neither should he eat"* (2 Thess. 3:10b). So, God will direct you to work, but even though you work, don't start seeing yourself as the owner of what you've received. God is the one who has given you the increase (1 Cor. 3:7). He blesses you with every good thing in your life so that you can steward what He has given.

CHAPTER 2

PROSPERITY'S FIRST STEP

*He that is faithful in that which is least is faithful
also in much: and he that is unjust in the least is
unjust also in much.*

Luke 16:10

People use this scripture to say that if you want to be
entrusted with a lot of authority, then you have to start
small and work your way up. It isn't wrong to use this scripture to teach that truth; however, that isn't really what Jesus
was talking about here.

The context of a scripture determines its main application, and the context of this scripture is the steward who
had wasted his master's money. Jesus was saying that the
least area of trusting God is money. That's a big piece of
information! It is also completely contrary to the way most
believers think.

Many think that money is something for mature Christians to deal with and that salvation and living a holy life are the simple things. But finances are the least area of trusting God! It's a starting place. In the parable of the unjust steward, Jesus went on to say,

> *If therefore ye have not been faithful in the unrigh-teous mammon, who will commit to your trust the true riches? And if ye have not been faithful in that which is another man's, who shall give you that which is your own? No servant can serve two masters: for either he will hate the one, and love the other; or else he will hold to the one, and despise the other. Ye cannot serve God and mammon.*
>
> Luke 16:11–13

The point is, if you can't lift five pounds, then you certainly shouldn't go out and try to lift a hundred pounds. Jesus was calling mammon (money) "that which is least." If you aren't trusting God in your finances, then you are deceiving yourself to think you are trusting Him to restore your family, to receive healing in your body, or emotional healing. If you haven't started trusting God with your finances, how can you trust that you're born again?

To be clear, I am not saying that if you give money, you can receive salvation or a miracle. You can't buy anything from God. You can only receive from Him by faith. What I *am* saying is that using your faith for finances is the least use of faith; and if you haven't done that which is least, then you won't be able to do greater things. That is a profound principle!

THE RICH YOUNG RULER

Let's look at the story of the rich young ruler.

When he was gone forth into the way, there came one running, and kneeled to him, and asked him, Good Master, what shall I do that I may inherit eternal life?

Mark 10:17

Sometimes we read through Scripture without thinking about it enough to let it have its full impact on us. Picture the situation here. Jesus was a radical and controversial figure in His day. The scribes and Pharisees had established that anyone who acknowledged Jesus as the Messiah was going to be kicked out of the synagogue (John 9:22), so there was persecution for those who associated with Him.

This young man had some degree of commitment to fall down at Jesus' feet the way he did. But Jesus recognized that the young man wasn't all that he appeared to be. As it says in 1 Samuel 16:7, ". . . *man [looks] on the outward appearance, but the Lord [looks] on the heart.*" So, Jesus told the young man to keep the commandments, and the young man had the nerve to say that he had kept them all from his youth (Mark 10:20). Nobody has ever observed all of the commandments (Rom. 3:23)! He was deceiving himself to think he had kept them. Look how Jesus responded:

> *Then Jesus beholding him loved him, and said unto him, One thing thou lackest: go thy way, sell whatsoever thou hast, and give to the poor, and thou shalt have treasure in heaven: and come, take up the cross, and follow me.*
>
> Mark 10:21

Jesus loved the young man, and He didn't say these things because He was mad or to drive him away. In his heart, this man was trusting in money, and Jesus was trying to help him shift his trust to God.

When the young man heard Jesus ask him to sell everything he had and give the proceeds to the poor, he hung his head and walked away. He knew in his heart that he couldn't do it. After the man left, the disciples began asking Jesus questions about what had just happened. Finally, Jesus said to them,

Verily I say unto you, There is no man that hath left house, or brethren, or sisters, or father, or mother, or wife, or children, or lands, for my sake, and the gospel's, But he shall receive an hundredfold now in this time, houses, and brethren, and sisters, and mothers, and children, and lands, with persecutions; and in the world to come eternal life.

Mark 10:29–30

In other words, if the man had sold everything he had and given it to the poor, he would have received a hundred-fold return in this life. Jesus wasn't trying to take from him. He would have blessed the man back a hundred times over! Yes, we're stewards, and the money we have isn't really ours, but God is never going to let us out-give Him. When we do give, the Lord will always bless us back—not just in heaven but here on earth too.

The rich man's refusal to sell his possessions revealed the true condition of his heart. Money was his god. Likewise, if some of the things I am saying rub you the wrong way, it may be that your heart isn't right in this matter. Just as Jesus used money to reveal the rich man's attitude, you can see what is in a person's heart by looking at how they operate financially.

Trust the Source

Jesus didn't ask every rich person He met to sell everything they owned. He went to the house of a very wealthy tax collector named Zacchaeus and never mentioned money—and tax collectors earned a lot of money by stealing from people (Luke 19:2–9)! Zacchaeus decided to give half of his goods to the poor and to restore four times any money he had stolen, but Jesus didn't ask him to do those things. Jesus didn't ask everyone to sell all they had because the issue isn't whether you have money—it's whether money has you. Are you trusting money instead of God?

This message isn't just for the mature believer. Even "baby Christians" should start with trusting God in their finances because until they can trust Him to be their source, they won't have the confidence to step out and do the things He's called them to do.

Sometimes we're afraid to step out and do what God is leading us to do, but the blessing on our lives comes from doing what God has called us to do. When my wife Jamie and I really started to step out and trust God with our finances, we saw the Lord come through for us time and time again. I could easily spend hours telling stories of God's miraculous provision in my life. I'm telling you, when we started trusting God with our finances, we not only began to see God's supernatural supply there but in other areas as well. I believe an important part of seeing my son raised from the dead, and the countless other miracles, was learning to trust God in the area of finances. If I hadn't done that which is least, I couldn't have seen those greater things come to pass. That can be true for you too.

CHAPTER 3

THE UNJUST STEWARD

I mentioned the parable of the unjust steward in the last chapter, but now I want to take a closer look at what Jesus was teaching. This parable is one of the hardest to understand. But if you can get a revelation of this parable, it will make a big difference in the way you view and use money. The parable starts like this:

> And [Jesus] said also unto his disciples, There was a certain rich man, which had a steward; and the same was accused unto him that he had wasted his goods. And he called him, and said unto him, How is it that I hear this of thee? give an account of thy stewardship; for thou mayest be no longer steward.
>
> Luke 16:1–2

This parable tells of a wealthy man who had someone managing his money. The man found out that the steward was mismanaging his funds; so he told the steward to get his books in order.

> *Then the steward said within himself, "What shall I do? for my lord taketh away from me the steward-ship: I cannot dig; to beg I am ashamed.*

Luke 16:3

It's probably not true that he couldn't dig. It is probably more accurate to say he *wouldn't* dig. This raises a good point: Not everyone who has financial problems is lazy, but lazy people usually have financial problems. They're looking for a get-rich-quick scheme or some other kind of shortcut. That's not how God's system works. Even if you were to defy the odds and strike it rich, Scripture says that wealth obtained through vanity doesn't last (Prov. 13:11). Prosperity isn't about getting money any way you can; there is a right and a wrong way to do it.

So, after concluding that he didn't want to look for work, the steward said, "I am ashamed to beg." It's too bad he wasn't ashamed to steal—he might still have a job! But since he wouldn't work or beg, he landed on an idea he liked:

> *I am resolved what to do, that, when I am put out of the stewardship, they may receive me into their*

houses. So he called every one of his lord's debtors unto him, and said unto the first, How much owest thou unto my lord? And he said, An hundred measures of oil. And he said unto him, Take thy bill, and sit down quickly, and write fifty. Then said he to another, And how much owest thou? And he said, An hundred measures of wheat. And he said unto him, Take thy bill, and write fourscore.

Luke 16:4–7

This steward was too lazy to work and too proud to beg, so he kept on stealing money. But instead of putting the money into his own pocket, he put the money in the pockets of people who owed his master money. The logic behind this was that when the steward got fired, he could go back to all of those debtors and say, "Hey, remember how I saved you thousands of dollars? Well, I'm out of work now. Can you give me a hand?" All of those people would feel indebted to him, or responsible for his unemployment, and he could "mooch" off of them instead of getting a job.

Up until this point in the parable, it's not too difficult to understand what's going on. What's unusual about this story is how the master responded:

And the lord commended the unjust steward, because he had done wisely: for the children of this world are in their generation wiser than the children of light.

Luke 16:8

The simple fact that the master found something to commend this unjust steward says a lot about the master's attitude toward money. Would you pay compliments to someone you caught stealing from you? If you came home one night and found a thief standing in your living room with a pillowcase full of your valuables, having bypassed your security system, would you say to him, "Wow, you did a great job"? Or, like most, would you be angry and get justice?

It's possible that the master was so rich that he didn't care if people stole from him, but I doubt it. If he didn't care about his money, he wouldn't have called the steward to account in the first place. I think this master understood that money is a tool, as I've mentioned previously. Why? Because he understood that money is not what we are meant to value. It is the blessing and favor of God that make us rich.

Most people judge their worth by their savings and retirement fund, but those things are just a physical manifestation of the real asset—God's favor. Wealth is just a by-product of God's favor. The Lord told Abraham, *"I will bless thee, and make thy name great; and thou shalt be a blessing"* (Gen. 12:2b). It was the spoken favor of God on Abraham's life that caused him to prosper. The master in Luke 16 obviously had a revelation that his true wealth was the favor of God, not the money the steward was stealing.

This goes back to the first point I made about being a steward and recognizing that everything we have comes from God. The Lord gives us resources, but they aren't our real asset. The true treasure is the blessing and the favor of God that *produces* the resources. This is one reason Scripture reminds us that the power to get wealth comes from God (Deut. 8:18). It's the blessing and the favor of God on you that is the real asset!

MONEY IS A TOOL

The other important reason the rich master commended the unjust steward was because the steward harnessed the true power of money. Instead of pocketing the stolen money, the steward was using it to prepare for his future. Again, money is a tool. Jesus said,

> *Make to yourselves friends of the mammon of unrighteousness; that, when ye fail, they may receive you into everlasting habitations.*

> Luke 16:9

The Greek word translated as *fail* here also means "death" or "die."[1] This scripture is telling us to use money, which is temporal and perishes (1 Pet. 1:7), and to make friends who will receive us into everlasting habitations when we die. In other words, by investing money in the lives of others, we can take something that is destined for destruction (2 Pet. 3:10) and turn it into something eternal. If we sow it into the Gospel and touch other people's lives, those people will be lined up in heaven to thank us for the way we helped them in this life.

The purpose of this parable is to show us that the best use of money isn't on temporary things that are going to pass away. Prosperity isn't about your house or car. It's not about having the latest gadgets and the fanciest clothes. The number one use of your money is to touch people's lives.

A lot of people who have put their trust in money won't even make it to heaven, but I also believe there are Christians who won't have much treasure waiting in heaven. They'll still be blessed and overwhelmed by the love of God because no one is saved according to works. However, there won't be anybody waiting to welcome them into heaven because they never used their money to impact anybody.

Just because I'm saying not to trust in money doesn't mean God wants you to be poor. He is not against you taking care of yourself. What I'm saying is that your attitude about money will change when you really get a revelation of prosperity. You'll be thinking, *How little money do I need to take care of my family, and how much can I invest on eternity?* No believer will be saying, "Oh, I sure wish I'd spent my money on a nicer car or a third television." No way! It's only what you give away that you get to keep. No one is foolish enough to not give away something they can't keep in order to get something they can't lose.

When the master told the steward he was going to be fired, the steward finally got the message that he had better start planning for the future. He realized that he needed to take the money he had access to and use its influence and power to invest in his future.

The two main points we learn from the parable of the dishonest steward are that money is not our greatest asset, and wise people invest their money for the future. Remember, the blessing of God is what makes you rich, not money. As long as you have God's blessing, wealth will always find and even overtake you. The key is learning not to spend all your money on short-lived pleasures but to help invest in eternity. Then, someday, multitudes of people will be waiting to welcome you into heaven.

Chapter 4

Prosperity Isn't Selfish

Selfishness is the most prevalent attitude today. A lot of people are making their decisions based purely upon whatever is best for them. If something promotes their personal well-being, then it's good—if not, then it's bad. They don't have any reference larger than their own needs. They think that prosperity is selfish. I've had lots of people tell me they are satisfied with what they have, and they don't want any more. I agree that being content with what you have is godly, but it's also selfish to say you don't want more resources. What most of those people are really saying is, "As long as my needs are met, then I'm satisfied." This is the wrong application to what Paul was saying in his first letter to Timothy:

> *But godliness with contentment is great gain. For we brought nothing into this world, and it is certain we can carry nothing out. And having food and raiment let us be therewith content. But they that will be rich fall into temptation and a snare, and into*

many foolish and hurtful lusts, which drown men in destruction and perdition. For the love of money is the root of all evil: which while some coveted after, they have erred from the faith, and pierced themselves through with many sorrows.

1 Timothy 6:6–10

Some people have taken these verses to mean that money in itself is evil, but the word *contentment* in this passage is talking about having your needs met. It isn't saying that a godly attitude means you can't have riches. You can have both if your motive is right. Loving God doesn't mean you have to be poor, and having money doesn't mean you are ungodly. For one thing, wealth is relative. Some of the people preaching that you can't have money and still be a servant of God are extremely wealthy by the world's standards. We are super rich compared to the people Paul was writing about in this passage. Here in America, we have conveniences they couldn't have dreamed of: running hot water, air conditioning, indoor plumbing, microwaves, cars, and homes fit for kings. We are living in a time of prosperity unlike any in all of history.

This passage of Scripture isn't saying we can't have money. It says the *love* of money is the root of all evil—not money itself. Money isn't the problem; it's the attitude that people have toward money. It's putting your trust in money and finding your fulfillment in it. If you just put your trust in God, then He will get the money to you to accomplish His instructions and the call He has placed on your life. The problem comes when you love money and what it will produce more than you love God, and when you rely on it instead of looking to Him as your source.

God will bless you so that you can be a blessing to those in need. Without extra finances, you are limited in your ability to do that. It's better to prosper and increase your finances—not for yourself but so you can be a blessing to someone else. Scripture says,

> And God is able to make all grace abound toward you; that ye, always having all sufficiency in all things, may abound to every good work.

> 2 Corinthians 9:8

EATERS AND SOWERS

> Now he that ministereth seed to the sower both minister bread for your food, and multiply your seed sown, and increase the fruits of your righteousness.

> 2 Corinthians 9:10

This verse isn't really about farming; it's an illustration of a spiritual principle. A single kernel of corn planted in the ground will sprout up a plant that bears thousands of kernels of corn. When you give money away, it's like planting a seed. In the same way that planting a seed gives rise to a new plant that bears many more seeds, giving money away causes finances to grow in your life.

According to this scripture, God gives seed to the sower—just like God gave Isaac a hundredfold return on the crop he planted during a drought (Gen. 26:12). The people who abandoned their fields and ran off to Egypt in search of prosperity didn't receive anything. God gave the return to Isaac because he sowed. God prospers people if they are givers.

We also are told in God's Word, "For the eyes of the Lord run to and fro throughout the whole earth, to shew himself strong in the behalf of them whose heart is perfect toward him" (2 Chron. 16:9a). The word *perfect* here means "complete," "whole," and "at peace."[2]

It isn't talking about being sinless; it's talking about having a mature heart with a right attitude toward God. The Lord is searching the earth, looking for the kind of people who will give genuinely, from the heart—not as a form of manipulation or just giving to get. I tell you, when

God finds these people, He will get finances to them. These are people He sees as having the correct attitude about stewardship.

You could turn it around and say it this way: If you are consistently short on money—if you always have more month than you have money—then maybe God doesn't see you as a giver, as a good steward. That's not the only reason for experiencing lack. Other things could be going on to cause lack in your life, but it's also possible that your heart isn't right.

There are two dominant heart conditions when it comes to money: eaters and sowers. *Eaters* are the ones who are all about getting their own needs met. They are seeking to establish their own kingdoms. They use their resources to buy everything they want, and they only give when there is something left over. *Sowers*, on the other hand, are all about putting other people first. Sowers need to eat too, of course, but their hearts' desire is to give and seek God's kingdom first. *Sowers* are the people God is searching the world to find.

When we understand finances properly, we realize that prosperity isn't about us; it's about being able to bless other people. I'm telling you, being a sower is the key to prosperity! It's counterintuitive. Selfishness short-circuits prosperity because it causes us to consume all of our resources. It turns us into a vacuum cleaner that sucks up everything in sight. We ought to be just the opposite. Christians should be like leaf blowers: giving money left and right. We should be imitating God by searching for opportunities to give and asking Him to show us how we can be a blessing.

Another thing to keep in mind is that prosperity doesn't happen overnight. You don't go from being selfish to becoming a generous millionaire instantly. There are a couple of reasons for that. First, there is a time between planting seed and harvesting. Fruit doesn't show up the next day. It's seed, *time*, and harvest (Gen. 8:22). Second, money has power; and you might not be able to handle the power of prosperity right away.

God knows you have needs, and He wants you to be taken care of. Remember, He doesn't mind if you live in a nice house and drive a nice car, as long as you aren't consuming all your finances on yourself. When you get the attitude of a giver and walk it out over time, He will cause you to prosper. If God can get money through you, He'll get it to you—and it won't be long before you have plenty left over for yourself.

CHAPTER 5

THE TITHE

We have been redeemed from the curse of the Law, and we aren't under the bondage of legalism to tithing, but we should also recognize that tithing was a biblical principle before the Law came along. Abraham wasn't living under the Law, yet he tithed (Gen. 14:20). However, the main passage people use to teach on the tithe is out of Malachi 3. Let's read what it says.

> *Will a man rob God? Yet ye have robbed me. But ye say, Wherein have we robbed thee? In tithes and offerings. Ye are cursed with a curse: for ye have robbed me,* even *this whole nation. Bring ye all the tithes into the storehouse, that there may be meat in mine house, and prove me now herewith, saith the LORD of hosts, if I will not open you the windows of heaven, and pour you out a blessing, that* there shall *not* be room *enough* to receive it. *And I will rebuke the devourer for your sakes, and he shall not destroy the fruits of your ground; neither shall your*

vine cast her fruit before the time in the field, saith
the LORD *of hosts.*

Malachi 3:8–11

Nearly everyone who teaches on the tithe cites this passage. Usually, it is used like a club to beat people into submission to give at least a tenth of their finances. But there is a huge difference between the punishment that came for disobeying the Law under the Old Covenant and the grace that we live under in the New Covenant. The main motivation for tithing today should be out of love for God because He first loved us (1 John 4:19) and out of love for people, to bless them. We don't tithe in an attempt to keep the Law. As a matter of fact, we shouldn't even try.

For as many as are of the works of the law are under
the curse: for it is written, Cursed is every one that
continueth not in all things which are written in the
book of the law to do them.

Galatians 3:10

You are cursed if you don't keep all of the Law. You can't just keep some of it, or do the best you can, and think God will make up the difference. No, if you don't keep every letter of the Law, then you are cursed! This is why Jesus came. You are absolutely incapable of keeping the Law.

It's impossible. The people who are trying to say you are cursed if you don't tithe are missing this point. You either trust the grace of God, or you reject Jesus' sacrifice and put your trust in your own performance, forfeiting God's grace. You have to be 100 percent perfect—never making a single mistake in thought, word, or deed for your entire life—or you have to humble yourself and receive the gift of God's grace. Trying to satisfy the Law by paying a tithe isn't going to help.

> *But that no man is justified by the law in the sight of God, it is evident: for, The just shall live by faith. And the law is not of faith: but, The man that doeth them shall live in them. Christ hath redeemed us from the curse of the law, being made a curse for us.*
>
> Galatians 3:11–13a

Yes, we have been redeemed from the curse of the Law! This passage couldn't be any clearer. It's true that the verse in Malachi 3 says we *"are cursed with a curse"* if we don't tithe—but this is exactly what we have been redeemed from. The whole attitude that God is going to punish us for not paying a tithe is completely unscriptural. The church I went to as a child used to tell us that if we didn't pay our tithes, God would take it from us in doctors' bills. That's not the truth!

I'm telling you, God doesn't relate to us that way under the New Covenant. Christ freed us from the curse of the Law. God is not coming against you. He is not going to take money from you if you don't tithe. Trying to pay off God like He's some kind of mobster is the wrong motivation. You're not going to benefit from that kind of giving and motivation.

It's also worth mentioning that the passage in Malachi 3:8–11 says the curse comes by robbing God in tithes *and* offerings. The ministers who use this verse to teach about tithing from a Law perspective conveniently overlook that you also have to give offerings to keep the Law. I've never personally sat down and figured it out, but I've heard other ministers say that the offerings added up to way more than the tithe. There were so many offerings that, altogether, the mandatory giving totaled more like 33 percent of everything you bring in. So, if you are trying to live by the Law, you are cursed unless you are giving at least that percentage.

I've had a number of people criticize me over teaching that we aren't under the curse when we don't tithe, but they don't have anything to say when I point out that Malachi 3 mentions tithes *and* offerings. I can guarantee you that most of the people who are so adamant about the curse of the tithe are not giving 33 percent. But it's hypocritical to say you are cursed for not paying tithes and just leave the offerings out. Christ has redeemed us from the curse of the Law, so we're not cursed under the New Covenant for not tithing.

Now let's look at some benefits to tithing.

BENEFITS TO TITHING

Just because the punishment for not tithing has been taken away doesn't mean we should stop giving. It's similar to how parents teach children to do the right thing by using punishment, or the threat of it, to keep their kids in line. I grew up on a busy road, and my mother would threaten to spank me if I ever crossed the street without looking both ways. Actually, she spanked me a number of times! She did it because she loved me, and she didn't want me getting hit by a car. My mother isn't around to spank me anymore, but I still look both ways before crossing the street because it's the smart thing to do.

A long time ago, a man heard me preach on how giving out of fear of punishment profits you nothing, and he decided to change how he was giving. He was the kind who wrote out his tithe check down to the penny. The bottom line was that he was tithing because he felt obligated to give God 10 percent of his income, or else. At the time, he was making around $3,000 a month, which was a lot of money back then, but he still felt like he was always behind financially. So, after hearing me teach, he and his wife decided they were going to start giving as they purposed in their hearts, out of joy, realizing that *"God loveth a cheerful giver"* (2 Cor. 9:7b). He stopped calculating his tithe exactly, and they just started giving whatever they wanted.

About six months later, he realized that they had more money in the bank than they'd ever had before. His first thought was, *I bet I've decreased my giving.* Prior to his change of heart, he paid his tithe like a bill. He put it in the same column as all of his other debts and paid it every month like clockwork. By his thinking, extra money in his account meant he must not have been paying his "tithing bill." So, he went back and added together his checks over the past six months to see how much he had been giving. What he discovered surprised him: He had moved his giving up to 24 percent of his income. He was giving more than twice as much as he ever had, yet he was more prosperous than ever—because God was prospering him supernaturally.

When you give grudgingly or of necessity, or because you think God is going to break your kneecaps if you don't pay up, it profits you nothing. You get zero benefit from that kind of giving. The people you give to will benefit, but it isn't going to come back to you. That kind of giving won't influence your future. You have to come out from under the mindset of Old Covenant obligation and start giving with a joyful heart if you want to see a return on your giving.

The Right Motivation

Since the wrong motivation voids our giving, it would be better to give God one percent or two percent cheerfully than to give 10 percent with the wrong attitude. As I mentioned earlier, we need to give because we love God and we love people. Love is the main motivation. But we also need to give because we trust God. God wants us to prove Him to see if we don't get a return when we give with the right motive. We saw earlier that the Lord talked about this saying,

> *Bring ye all the tithes into the storehouse, that there may be meat in mine house, and prove me now herewith, saith the* Lord *of hosts, if I will not open you the windows of heaven, and pour you out a blessing, that* there shall *not* be room *enough* to receive it.
>
> Malachi 3:10

As far as I know, this is the only instance in Scripture where the Lord says, *"prove me."* Basically, He's saying, "Try it, and see if it doesn't work!" Nearly everything else He said was a command: Thou shalt do this, or thou shalt *not* do that. But when it comes to tithing, He said *"prove me."* I think He said it this way because He knows of the perceived risk of taking a portion of what we need to survive and giving it away. When you are dependent upon money to pay bills and buy food, it could be hard at first to put your trust in a God you can't see. He is aware of this, so He's saying, "Try Me." Now, it's not that God needs your money, but you need to trust Him.

If you need to lower your giving until your faith can build up and you can give at least 10 percent with a good heart, then do it. But eventually, you want to get to where you are thinking, *God, this is Your money. What do You want me to do with it?* It all comes down to the motive of your heart.

I encourage you to give and to tithe, but don't do it out of fear or guilt; do it because you love God and because you want to trust Him with what He has given you. When you purify your motives for tithing and start doing it as you desire in your heart, I believe that then you'll begin to see the hundredfold return on your giving—and you'll probably find yourself wanting to give a lot more than 10 percent.

CHAPTER 6

PARTNERSHIP

GIVE WHERE YOU'RE FED

It matters where you give—where you plant your seed. Some people think they reap a benefit from their giving regardless of what the church does with their money, but that's not true. You'd be a very poor farmer with that kind of attitude. You can't expect the same results from casting your seed on pavement that you would get from planting it in fertile soil. In addition, every time you give to a church or minister, you are casting a vote in support of how they conduct themselves and their ministry—whether it's good or bad; so it absolutely matters where you give your money.

Scripture says to bring our tithes into the storehouse, so you should be giving where you are spiritually fed. It's wrong to put your money into something that you don't agree with and then go get fed by ministries you don't support financially. That's like eating at a restaurant and going across the street to a different one to pay for your meal. No, you pay your bill where you ate—and you should give your tithe where you get spiritually fed. If you aren't being fed at your church, then you shouldn't be tithing there.

The return on your giving is going to depend, to a degree, on how fruitful the ground is that you are sowing into. It's the difference between planting in concrete and fertile soil. If you give to a church or ministry that isn't really accomplishing the Lord's work (concrete), then you are going to get marginal returns. When you plant your seed in a place that is fruitful and ministering the Word of God (fertile soil), then you are going to receive a better return. Don't give where you are begged or pressured, or where you've always given—give where you are fed. Bring the tithes into the storehouse! Wherever you get your "food" from is where you should be giving; it's really that simple.

However, we also need to keep in mind that giving where we are fed can't be the only criteria for our giving. If that were the only reason for giving, then missionaries who work in faraway countries wouldn't have any income, and no one would be helping widows and orphans. The people that missionaries help are often impoverished and unable to support them. Missionaries need financial partners who will help them spread the Gospel but who don't directly benefit from their ministry. So, giving where we are fed isn't the only guideline for tithing, but I believe it should be the primary one.

A good local church will feed us in ways that no other ministry can. The body of Christ is dependent upon the local church. If we didn't have local churches to meet our needs and we were solely dependent upon television preachers (like me), then the body of Christ would be in a crisis situation. The local church is the backbone of the body, and it is best for every one of us to be in a good local church where we can give our tithes—but we shouldn't put our tithes into a dead church.

DEAD CHURCHES AND CHARLATAN PREACHERS

In the first place, if you are in a dead church, then get out! Go find yourself a church that is preaching the Gospel, and then put your tithe into that church and use offerings to support other parts of the body of Christ. Maybe you live in a rural area with limited options, or your spouse will only go to one certain church or something else keeps you tied to a church that isn't preaching the Gospel. If for some reason you can't find a good local church or get out of the dead one you're in, then, at a minimum, you shouldn't give all of your money there. The best option is to get out of the dead church, but if you can't—or won't—then you should at least split your tithe.

This principle of giving where you are fed is really simple, and it would solve a lot of problems if believers followed it. The preachers who are lying and manipulating people in order to get their money are not truly feeding the body of Christ. They will go out of business if we'd just stop giving them money. They'd have to come up with some other con and move on with their lives. Then the people who are really feeding Christians would be getting all of the resources, and we would have an abundance of finances. The good churches wouldn't have to hold car washes and bake sales to raise money.

We're supposed to give as we purpose in our own hearts—and not where we are coerced, intimidated, condemned, or begged. I hate to say it, but I believe the majority of giving in the body of Christ is in response to begging or some sort of emotional coercion. Some preachers are raising a lot of money by manipulating people and doing all kinds of ungodly things, and it bothers me that Christians fall for that. The body of Christ is empowering those preachers and perpetuating all of that manipulation by giving money to support it. It's possible for some good to come out of that kind of giving because God can use anything, but those practices are wrong. If—and this is a big if—the church would learn the biblical guidelines for when and why to give, then we would starve out the charlatans. The people who are truly preaching the Word of God would have such an abundance that they would not have to mention money as often.

Your Partnership in the Kingdom

One of the best-known scriptures about prosperity is the apostle Paul's statement to the Philippians: *"But my God shall supply all your need..."* (Phil. 4:19). You'll hear that verse taught like it applies to every person on the face of the planet. It's true that God wants to supply all of your needs, and there are plenty of scriptures that talk about that—like how God provides for the birds of the air and the lilies of the field (Matt. 6:25–30). But Paul wrote this particular verse about people who gave where they had been fed by partnering with him in the Gospel. Earlier in his letter, Paul wrote,

> *I thank my God upon every remembrance of you, always in every prayer of mine for you all making request with joy, for your fellowship in the gospel from the first day until now.*
>
> Philippians 1:3–5

The word translated *fellowship* is the Greek word *koinonia*, and it means "partnership."[3] Paul was thanking the Philippians for their partnership. He saw that their giving would cause God to pour out a blessing on them and result in a hundredfold return:

*Notwithstanding ye have well done, that ye did com-
municate with my affliction. Now ye Philippians
know also, that in the beginning of the gospel, when
I departed from Macedonia, no church communicated with me as concerning giving and receiving,
but ye only.*

Philippians 4:14–15

When he says *communicated*, Paul is talking about how they gave financially. The amazing thing here is that he said no other churches had given him money to help preach the Gospel—only the Philippians! Paul and his companions were in constant jeopardy, and they endured great persecution and suffering to spread the Good News. But none of the other churches Paul started supported him in his work. That's tragic!

It seems that people gave to Paul only while he was in town preaching. They fed him and gave him a place to stay, but as soon as he left, he was on his own again. So, every time he went to a new place, he had to start all over financially. I don't think Paul should have been scraping by like that. People should have been so thankful for what God was doing through him and how he had sown into their lives that they took care of him no matter where he was. You can see why Paul was thankful every time he thought about the Philippians.

For even in Thessalonica ye sent once and again unto my necessity. Not because I desire a gift: but I desire fruit that may abound to your account.

Philippians 4:16–17

"*Once and again*" just means they sent money to Paul more than once. He understood that their consistent giving would result in a supernatural return because God gives seed to sowers (2 Cor. 9:10). Paul talked about how their giving caused him to abound, and *then* he wrote,

But my God shall supply all your need according to his riches in glory by Christ Jesus.

Philippians 4:19

There is no doubt that God delights in the prosperity of His servants, or that He sends sun and rain on the just and the unjust alike (Ps. 35:27; Matt. 5:45; and 3 John 2). He desires to bless both believers and unbelievers, but this particular verse in Philippians 4 is talking about people who weren't just giving to Paul because they were receiving from him; they were giving so that people beyond their town would receive from him. That's powerful!

Philippians 4:19 is talking about the special blessing on those who become partners in spreading the Gospel, which means that if you really want to be blessed, then partner with a ministry that has a big vision and is doing a great job of spreading the Gospel. The way God gets money to a ministry is by giving it to the believers who support it. In order for the money to get to the ministry, it has to pass through the hands of partners first; "and as the money passes through, there will be plenty left over for you." So, one of the best ways to prosper is to find a ministry that is powerfully anointed by God and become a partner with it.

I couldn't provide one week's worth of the income it takes to run my ministry. It takes the support of our partners to supply the ministry's financial needs and enable me to do what God has called me to do. I know that our partners have to prosper before I can, so I pray that God blesses our partners and causes them to abound. My ability to accomplish God's will upon my life is directly dependent upon other people joining with me and becoming partners. The same is true for every other ministry out there.

When you're a partner, God causes a supernatural flow of finances to be directed toward you. Let me reiterate: He has made provision for *every* believer, but there is a special anointing upon people who give in order to help spread the Gospel. When you say, "I want to help this church change our city" or "I want to help this person go around the world and spread the Gospel," then God can prosper you to do that. He gives money to sowers, who will plant their seed in ministries that advance the kingdom (Deut. 8:18). And He always gives more than enough so there is plenty left over for them.

Aside from causing a flow of finances to pass through partners' hands, there is an additional benefit to partnering with a ministry.

THE FLOW OF BLESSING

A man's gift maketh room for him, and bringeth him before great men.

Proverbs 18:16

I used to think this scripture meant *gift* in the sense of God-given ability or anointing. I thought that if I would use my gift of teaching properly, for instance, it would open up doors and bring me before important, influential men and women. But the Hebrew word used for *gift* here is *matan*, and it literally means "present."[4] It's clear from the other uses in Scripture that it means some kind of monetary gift (Prov. 15:27, 19:6).

In a negative sense, you could understand this kind of gift to be a bribe, but there is also a positive side to it. You can turn away wrath with a gift or gain favor with others. Gifts also have an effect in the spiritual realm. When you give, it opens up doors for you. It can create opportunities and bring you before powerful people. This is different from a bribe, and the story of queen of Sheba coming before King Solomon is a great example of a gift being used in this positive sense.

Solomon was the wisest and wealthiest man on the face of the earth. The Bible says that people came from all over the world to inquire of him and search out his wisdom (1 Kgs. 10:24). Think about that. I believe Solomon had more fame and notoriety than you could imagine the leader of any country having nowadays.

When the queen heard how wise and prosperous Solomon was, she traveled to Jerusalem to witness it for herself. She brought gifts to gain Solomon's attention and gain access to him. Scripture tells us that she went up *"with a very great train"* of camels bearing spices, precious stones, and *"very much gold"* (1 Kgs. 10:2). The queen was astounded by what she saw in King Solomon's court:

> *She gave the king an hundred and twenty talents of gold, and of spices very great store, and precious stones: there came no more such abundance of spices....*

> 1 Kings 10:10

A talent is equal to about 75.5 pounds, so that means she gave Solomon 9,000 pounds, or 145,000 ounces, of gold. I can guarantee a gift that size is going to make room for you. I don't know how long the line of people waiting to see King Solomon was, but the queen's gift moved her right to the front. Not only did she get to spend a little time with him, but she ate with him and saw all the different aspects of his kingdom. The implication is that she was able to spend a number of days with Solomon. We don't know the exact details, but the queen's gift brought her before the greatest man of her day—that's the positive power of a gift.

I'm sure some people were thinking, *Why give so much money to King Solomon? Think of how many poor people she could help with that money.* She could have changed entire nations with that money. She could have built buildings and helped farmers in every town she passed through. But the queen of Sheba decided she was going to use that money to go find out how King Solomon had become so successful in running his kingdom, then she could apply that knowledge to improving her own land. She probably passed up beggars and others in need who could have used her resources. But she gave to Solomon because she wanted to partake of the success he was experiencing, and it worked.

In a spiritual sense, when you partner with a ministry, your gifts make room for you. It's like you start drawing on the anointing that is on the ministry. You end up partaking of the fruits of the ministry. When you partner with someone who is preaching the Good News, then you receive the benefit of prospering from their blessing.

And king Solomon gave unto the queen of Sheba all her desire, whatsoever she asked, beside that which Solomon gave her of his royal bounty. So she turned and went to her own country, she and her servants.

1 Kings 10:13

The next verse tells us that Solomon received 666 talents of gold annually, plus the profits he made from businesses and the kings of other countries that paid him taxes—which means the queen's gift was only a fraction of King Solomon's yearly earnings. She ended up receiving more from Solomon than she gave! On her return journey, I believe the queen had tremendous wealth to use to aid beggars and farmers, but she also had wisdom and anointing she could use to build her entire nation.

That illustrates the point I'm trying to make: When you find someone who has reached a level of maturity, anointing, or prosperity that you want in your life, you need to start sowing into that good soil. You'll help get yourself to the same place. This is what the queen of Sheba did. She found a person who had more favor, more wisdom, and greater wealth, and she used a gift to gain access to him in order to glean these things for herself.

It's important to recognize that when you partner with a ministry, it opens a door to you where you begin partaking of the blessing and anointing that is on that ministry. Don't give just to get, but sow where you want to go. God will supernaturally meet your needs and also cause you to abound unto every good work (2 Cor. 9:8).

God won't let you out-give Him. He always blesses you back when you show faith in Him by giving of your substance. You will never be more faithful to God than He is to you. I'm not saying that partnering with a ministry is about giving just to get; that's why I spent so much time earlier talking about your heart motives being more important than the gift itself. But when your heart is right, partnering with a ministry to help it get the Gospel out is going to open up doors for you and cause you to prosper.

Giving is a powerful part of tapping into God's prosperity. Several different things help determine the harvest you get from your giving: the attitude you give with, where you give, and trusting God as your source; there isn't a formula. But you can't really prosper in God's economy until you start sowing into His kingdom. I recommend you do it regularly. That way, you won't spend your money before you can give and end up missing out on God's supernatural supply. As you become a deliberate, on-purpose giver—and you do it motivated by love—God's blessings will start to flow into your life and cause you to prosper like never before.

FURTHER STUDY

If you enjoyed this booklet and would like to learn more about some of the things I've shared, I suggest my teachings:

- *Financial Stewardship*
- *The Power of Partnership*
- *What's in Your Hand?*
- *A Sure Foundation*

These teachings are available for free at **awmi.net**, or they can be purchased at **awmi.net/store**.

Receive Jesus as Your Savior

Choosing to receive Jesus Christ as your Lord and Savior is the most important decision you'll ever make!

God's Word promises, *"That if thou shalt confess with thy mouth the Lord Jesus, and shalt believe in thine heart that God hath raised him from the dead, thou shalt be saved. For with the heart man believeth unto righteousness; and with the mouth confession is made unto salvation"* (Rom. 10:9–10). *"For whosoever shall call upon the name of the Lord shall be saved"* (Rom. 10:13). By His grace, God has already done everything to provide salvation. Your part is simply to believe and receive.

Pray out loud: "Jesus, I confess that You are my Lord and Savior. I believe in my heart that God raised You from the dead. By faith in Your Word, I receive salvation now. Thank You for saving me."

The very moment you commit your life to Jesus Christ, the truth of His Word instantly comes to pass in your spirit. Now that you're born again, there's a brand-new you!

Please contact us and let us know that you've prayed to receive Jesus as your Savior. We'd like to send you some free materials to help you on your new journey. Call our Helpline: **719-635-1111** (available 24 hours a day, seven days a week) to speak to a staff member who is here to help you understand and grow in your new relationship with the Lord.

Welcome to your new life!

RECEIVE THE HOLY SPIRIT

As His child, your loving heavenly Father wants to give you the supernatural power you need to live a new life. *"For every one that asketh receiveth; and he that seeketh findeth; and to him that knocketh it shall be opened...how much more shall* your *heavenly Father give the Holy Spirit to them that ask him?"* (Luke 11:10–13).

All you have to do is ask, believe, and receive!

Pray this: "Father, I recognize my need for Your power to live a new life. Please fill me with Your Holy Spirit. By faith, I receive it right now. Thank You for baptizing me. Holy Spirit, You are welcome in my life."

Some syllables from a language you don't recognize will rise up from your heart to your mouth (1 Cor. 14:14). As you speak them out loud by faith, you're releasing God's power from within and building yourself up in the spirit (1 Cor. 14:4). You can do this whenever and wherever you like.

It doesn't really matter whether you felt anything or not when you prayed to receive the Lord and His Spirit. If you believed in your heart that you received, then God's Word promises you did. *"Therefore I say unto you, What things soever ye desire, when ye pray, believe that ye receive* them, *and ye shall have* them" (Mark 11:24). God always honors His Word—believe it!

We would like to rejoice with you and help you understand more fully what has taken place in your life!

Please contact us to let us know that you've prayed to be filled with the Holy Spirit and to request the book *The New You & the Holy Spirit*. This book will explain in more detail about the benefits of being filled with the Holy Spirit and speaking in tongues. Call our Helpline: **719-635-1111** (available 24 hours a day, seven days a week).

CALL FOR PRAYER

If you need prayer for any reason, you can call our Helpline, 24 hours a day, seven days a week at **719-635-1111**. A trained prayer minister will answer your call and pray with you.

Every day, we receive testimonies of healings and other miracles from our Helpline, and we are ministering God's nearly-too-good-to-be-true message of the Gospel to more people than ever. So, I encourage you to call today!

About the Author

Andrew Wommack's life was forever changed the moment he encountered the supernatural love of God on March 23, 1968. As a renowned Bible teacher and author, Andrew has made it his mission to change the way the world sees God.

Andrew's vision is to go as far and deep with the Gospel as possible. His message goes far through the *Gospel Truth* television program, which is available to over half the world's population. The message goes deep through discipleship at Charis Bible College, headquartered in Woodland Park, Colorado. Founded in 1994, Charis has campuses across the United States and around the globe.

Andrew also has an extensive library of teaching materials in print, audio, and video. More than 200,000 hours of free teachings can be accessed at **awmi.net**.

Contact Information

Andrew Wommack Ministries, Inc.
PO Box 3333
Colorado Springs, CO 80934-3333
info@awmi.net
awmi.net

Helpline: 719-635-1111 (available 24/7)

Charis Bible College
info@charisbiblecollege.org
844-360-9577
CharisBibleCollege.org

For a complete list of our offices, visit
awmi.net/contact-us.

Connect with us on social media.

Andrew's LIVING COMMENTARY BIBLE SOFTWARE

Andrew Wommack's *Living Commentary* Bible study software is a user-friendly, downloadable program. It's like reading the Bible with Andrew at your side, sharing his revelation with you verse by verse.

Main features:
- Bible study software with a grace-and-faith perspective
- Over 26,000 notes by Andrew on verses from Genesis through Revelation
- *Matthew Henry's Concise Commentary*
- 12 Bible versions
- 2 concordances: *Englishman's Concordance* and *Strong's Concordance*
- 2 dictionaries: *Collaborative International Dictionary* and *Holman's Dictionary*
- Atlas with biblical maps
- Bible and *Living Commentary* statistics
- Quick navigation, including history of verses
- Robust search capabilities (for the Bible and Andrew's notes)
- "Living" (i.e., constantly updated and expanding)
- Ability to create personal notes

Whether you're new to studying the Bible or a seasoned Bible scholar, you'll gain a deeper revelation of the Word from a grace-and-faith perspective.

Purchase Andrew's *Living Commentary* today at **awmi.net/living**, and grow in the Word with Andrew.

Item code: 8350

ANDREW WOMMACK MINISTRIES